TOP 10 HOME RUN HITTERS

BY K. C. KELLEY

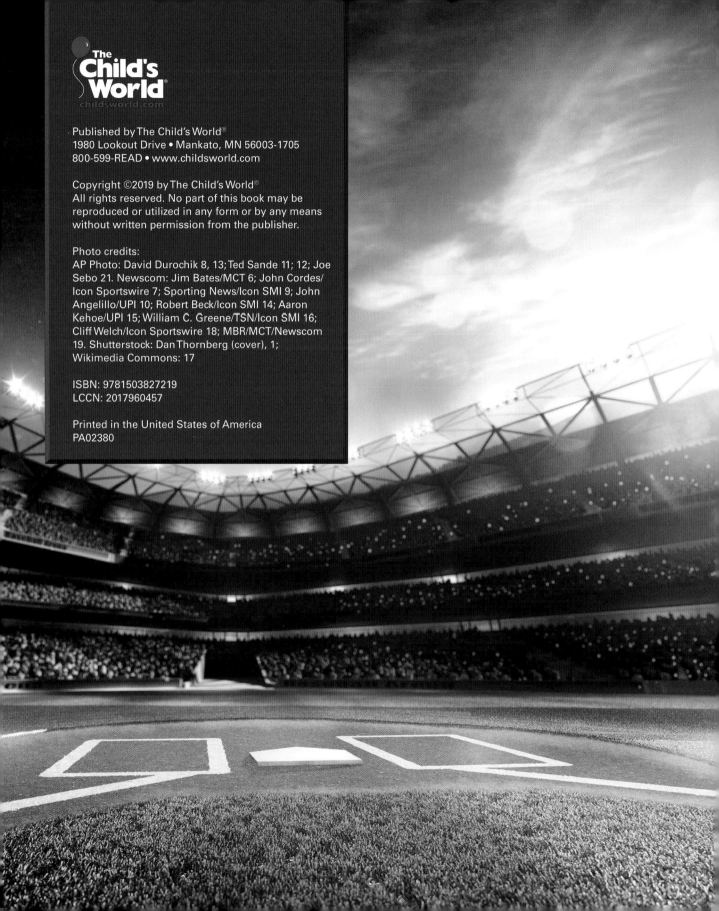

The Child's World®
childsworld.com

Published by The Child's World®
1980 Lookout Drive • Mankato, MN 56003-1705
800-599-READ • www.childsworld.com

Photo credits:
AP Photo: David Durochik 8, 13; Ted Sande 11; 12; Joe
Sebo 21. Newscom: Jim Bates/MCT 6; John Cordes/
Icon Sportswire 7; Sporting News/Icon SMI 9; John
Angelillo/UPI 10; Robert Beck/Icon SMI 14; Aaron
Kehoe/UPI 15; William C. Greene/TSN/Icon SMI 16;
Cliff Welch/Icon Sportswire 18; MBR/MCT/Newscom
19. Shutterstock: Dan Thornberg (cover), 1;
Wikimedia Commons: 17

ISBN: 9781503827219
LCCN: 2017960457

Printed in the United States of America
PA02380

CONTENTS

WHO'S NUMBER ONE?

At the end of a baseball game, everyone knows who won. It's the team with the most runs! At the end of the Major League season, the No. 1 team is clear—the winner of the World Series. Choosing the greatest home run hitter of all time is a bit harder. Is it the guy with the most homers? Or the player who hit them more often? Is it the hitter with the biggest homers? Fans, experts, and fellow players all have their opinions.

Opinions are different than facts. Facts are real things. Babe Ruth hit 714 home runs. That's a fact. Baseball is the greatest sport in the world. That's an opinion.

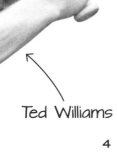

Ted Williams

NUMBERS, NUMBERS

Most Homers by Active Players

Through the 2017 season, these are the top five sluggers playing today:

1. Albert Pujols, 614

2. Adrian Beltre, 462

   Miguel Cabrera, 462

4. Ryan Howard, 382

5. Edwin Encarnacion, 348

(Note: Throughout this book, the stats you see are updated through 2017.)

It's 90 feet from home plate to first base. That's a fact. Fenway Park is the best place to watch a baseball game. That's an opinion. Some people might think baseball is not that great. (I know: Can you believe it?) But that's fine; that's their opinion. However, they can't say Ruth didn't hit 714 dingers. That's a fact. Red Sox fans think Fenway is No. 1. But you would find a very different opinion in lots of other big-league ballparks, where fans think THEIR place is No. 1.

Alex Rodriguez

And that's where *you* come in. You get to choose who is the greatest home run hitter ever. You will read lots of facts and stories about these great players. Based on that, what's your opinion? Who's No. 1? There are no wrong answers about who is the greatest home run hitter of all time . . . but you might have some fun discussions with your baseball-loving pals! Then again, you might just pick the guy with the MOST homers . . . it's up to you!

Read on and then after you're done, make up your own Top 10 list (find out more on page 20).

KEN GRIFFEY, JR.

MARINERS • REDS

How much did people love Ken Griffey, Jr.? He was elected to the Baseball Hall of Fame in 2016. He got 437 out of 440 votes. That was the highest **percentage** for any player . . . ever!

Even when he was a **veteran**, fans called him "The Kid." Griffey played with great joy and a love for the game. He started out in 1989 at only 19 for Seattle, following his dad to the Major Leagues. Griffey's first big plays were with his glove. In 1990, he won the first of his 10 **Gold Gloves** as a top fielder.

In 1993, he started slugging . . . and didn't stop! He smacked 45 homers that year and then led the AL with 40 in 1994. He hit a career-high 56 in 1997 and 1998. In his 22 big-league seasons, he had 15 seasons with 20 or more homers—that's called being consistent!

In 1990, Ken and his dad Ken Sr. were the first father and son to play in the same game!

NUMBERS, NUMBERS

Griffey is seventh all-time with 630 homers. He is third all-time among lefties, behind only Babe Ruth and Barry Bonds.

6

ALBERT PUJOLS

CARDINALS • ANGELS

Pujols was named the NL MVP in 2005, 2008, and 2009. He also finished second in MVP voting four times!

Few players have started out as well as Albert Pujols (POO-holz). Born in the Dominican Republic, he grew up in Kansas. In his rookie season with the Cardinals, he had 37 homers . . . and at least 30 in each of the next 11! In two of those seasons—2006 and 2011—he helped the Cardinals win the World Series.

Pujols is more than a slugger. He has a career **batting average** above .305. In eight seasons, he topped .320, and he led the NL in 2003 at .359.

In 2012, he signed with the Angels, where he had four seasons with 100 RBI. He's still going strong—he had 101 RBI in 2017 at age 37.

Off the field, Pujols is one of baseball's best guys. He and his family support children's charities.

NUMBERS, NUMBERS

Pujols is still slugging homers. Through 2017, he was in eighth place all-time with 614.

FRANK ROBINSON

REDS • ORIOLES

Frank Robinson might not be as famous as some other sluggers, but he was just as fearsome. With the Cincinnati Reds, he set an NL rookie record with 38 homers in 1956 and never stopped hitting them out of the park. Talk about being dependable: Robinson had at least 20 homers every season but one from 1956 to 1974! He was the NL **Most Valuable Player** (MVP) in 1961.

In 1966, the Reds surprised many people by trading Robinson to the Baltimore Orioles. The move didn't hurt his hitting. He was named the AL MVP after winning the **Triple Crown**. He became the first player ever to win the MVP award in both leagues. Robinson also played briefly with the Dodgers, Angels, and Indians.

In 1975, Robinson was named manager of the Cleveland Indians. He was the first African-American manager in big-league history.

Robinson won the Triple Crown by leading his league in home runs, runs batted in, and batting average. Only two players have accomplished it since Robinson!

NUMBERS, NUMBERS

Robinson hit 343 homers in the National League. He smacked 243 more during his time in the American League.

MIKE SCHMIDT

PHILLIES

Third base is a very hard position to play. It's called the "hot corner." Batters slam line drives and hard grounders right at you! It's so hard that being a top hitter while playing there is tough.

One player, though, is probably one of the best-fielding third basemen AND its No. 1 slugger. Mike Schmidt played 18 years for the Phillies and won nine Gold Gloves for his fielding. At the same time, he led the NL in homers eight times!

Schmidt's home run blasts were legendary. He always seemed to come up with the big blow when his team needed it most.

His career high was 48 homers in 1980. That was the year the Phillies won their first-ever World Series. Schmidt hit two homers and drove in seven runs and was named World Series MVP!

Schmidt was named the NL MVP in 1980, 1981, and 1986.

NUMBERS, NUMBERS
Schmidt's 548 career homers are the most ever by a third baseman.

ALEX RODRIGUEZ

MARINERS • RANGERS • YANKEES

The player known as "A-Rod" is a hero to some, and a villain to others. He had 696 home runs in 22 seasons. That's the fourth most ever. However, it turned out that for part of that time, he cheated. A-Rod was caught using drugs that helped him play better. Such drugs were against baseball rules.

In his first full season, 1996, he led the AL with a .358 batting average. He started really smacking homers with 42 in 1998. That was the first of six straight seasons with 40-plus dingers. His best was 57 in 2002, after he joined the Rangers.

He went on to join the Yankees and keep smacking homers. However, he was **banned** from baseball for the 2014 season after he admitted taking illegal drugs. He said it was for only two or three seasons, however. Should his whole career not count? Or was he a great slugger except for those seasons?

A-Rod was the AL MVP with Texas in 2003, and then again in 2005 and 2007 with the Yankees.

NUMBERS, NUMBERS

Here are A-Rod's top single-season home run totals:

57	2002
54	2007
52	2001
48	2005
47	2003

TED WILLIAMS

RED SOX

When Ted Williams was a teenager, he decided on his future. He said he would become "the greatest hitter who ever lived." A lot of experts would say that he made that dream come true.

Williams is the only player to win two Triple Crowns (1942 and 1947). In 1941, he batted .406, and was the last player in baseball history to reach the magical .400 mark. He was the AL batting champion six times, including a .388 mark in 1957 when he was 38 years old.

Williams won three MVP awards and finished second four times.

He hit plenty of homers, too. He led the AL four times and had at least 20 in every full season he played. He might have done even more. For parts of five seasons, he served America as a pilot in the Army and the Marines.

Williams had some great nicknames: Thumper, Teddy Ballgame, The Kid, and The Splendid Splinter.

NUMBERS, NUMBERS
Williams batted above .316 in every one of his full seasons except 1959.

WILLIE MAYS

GIANTS • METS

A slugger, a great fielder, a base stealer, and a batting champ: Willie Mays might just have been the best all-around player ever. He played at top speed for most of his 22 seasons, thrilling fans with diving catches and long homers.

He was the NL Rookie of the Year in 1951. He showed off his power early, with 20 homers. He topped that number in almost every other season until 1970! Mays did miss most of 1952 and all of 1953 while serving in the U.S. Army. The time off didn't hurt, though. He came back in 1954 to win the MVP and help the New York Giants win the World Series. Mays made the NL All-Star team that year. He would go on to play in a record-tying 24 All-Star Games.

Mays's first team was the New York Giants. They moved from New York City to San Francisco for the 1958 season. They joined the Los Angeles Dodgers as the first MLB teams in California.

In that 1954 Series, he made one of the most famous catches of all time. He sprinted to the centerfield wall, and with his back to the plate, snagged a long drive. In his career, this superstar won 12 Gold Gloves. That's tied for most ever by an outfielder.

In 1955, Mays had 51 homers to lead all of baseball and just kept slugging. Over the next decade, he not only crushed homers, but he used his great speed to steal bases. He is one of only a few players ever to lead their league in homers and steals.

In 1965, though aged 34, he had one of his best seasons, winning another MVP award after crushing 52 homers. Mays wrapped up his amazing career with two seasons with the Mets. In 1979, he was a shoo-in for the Baseball Hall of Fame. Many of today's top sluggers still meet with Mays for help from a homer hero!

NUMBERS, NUMBERS

Mays led the NL in just about every stat category at least once. Here are his league-leading best stats:

Avg.: .345 (1954)

HR: 52 (1965)

Runs: 129 (1961)

Hits: 190 (1960)

Stolen Bases: 40 (1956)

On-Base Percentage: .425 (1971)

BARRY BONDS

No one hit more homers than Barry Bonds. In 22 seasons, he crushed 762 long balls. In 2007, Bonds passed the great Hank Aaron, who had 755. Bonds also has the single-season record with 73 homers. He hit that many in 2001.

So why isn't he the obvious choice as the No. 1 home run hitter of all time? Because many people believe that he, like A-Rod, cheated. A-Rod was caught and admitted using illegal drugs. Bonds, however, has always said that he never did anything wrong. He never failed a drug test. However, most people did not believe him. In fact, he was put on trial for lying about it. But he was not convicted, so the mystery continues.

Here are the numbers. In his prime, Bonds was the greatest home run hitter ever. He had eight seasons with 40 or more homers.

Bonds is the only player in baseball history with more than 500 homers AND more than 500 steals. He is one of four players with 40 homers and 40 steals in a season. He had 42 and 40 in 2001.

From 2000 to 2004, he had 258 homers. That's a great *career* for many players! He also drove in runs in huge bunches; he had seven seasons with 110 or more RBI.

Even before he had big homer numbers, he was a superstar. He was the NL MVP for Pittsburgh in 1990 after hitting 33 homers and stealing 52 bases and winning a Gold Glove. He won the MVP again in 1992 and 1993. Few people think he was doing anything wrong then.

By 2001, though, many people suspected he was doing something he shouldn't. Still, with the Giants, he was the NL MVP four seasons in a row—2001 through 2004. That gave him seven MVP trophies, way more than any other player.

Bonds retired in 2007 after breaking Aaron's record. Did Bonds break the rules? Put it this way: He still has not been voted into the Hall of Fame. Best ever? You make the call.

NUMBERS, NUMBERS

On-base percentage (OBP) shows how often a batter reaches base by getting a hit, walking, or being hit by a pitch. Bonds was the king of OBP. In 2004, Bonds had a .609 OBP, the highest ever for a season. Slugging average shows a player's power. In 2001, Bonds had a .863 slugging average, also the highest ever.

BABE RUTH

RED SOX • YANKEES

Babe Ruth was baseball's first huge star. And he's almost as famous now as he was when he was playing. Before Ruth came along during World War I, very few homers were hit. After he started blasting long balls, baseball became a whole new ballgame. No one had ever hit like Ruth did, and only a few have come very close since.

Ruth actually began his career as a pitcher with the Boston Red Sox. He was one of the best **lefties** in the game. He helped the Red Sox win the World Series in 1916 and 1918. Even while pitching, he still led the AL with 11 homers in 1918. He broke the single-season record in 1919 with 29 homers.

In 1920, the sports world was shocked when Boston traded him to the New York Yankees.

Ruth had a ton of great nicknames—not just Babe. He was known as the Sultan of Swat, the Caliph of Clout, the Bambino, Bam, and the Big Fellow.

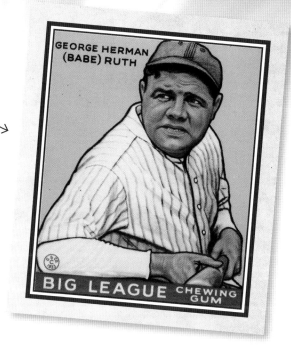

GEORGE HERMAN (BABE) RUTH

BIG LEAGUE CHEWING GUM

That's when his home run **binge** really began for the "Sultan of Swat." He smashed 54 in 1920. He topped his own mark with 59 in 1921. That was more homers than eight whole *teams* had that year! No one had ever seen a player like him. Baseballs flew high and far in every park he played in. Fans packed the seats to see the "Great Bambino" mash baseballs.

Ruth was not just great. He was MUCH greater than everyone else. When he hit 60 homers in 1927, his teammate Lou Gehrig was next with 47. No other players in the American League even hit 20! Ruth led the AL in homers 12 times. Perhaps bigger than his homers was his impact on baseball. His homers brought in millions of new fans. The sport became No. 1 in the country. Ruth's fun-loving personality also made him a huge star, even to people who didn't follow baseball.

Though some players have topped his home run totals, no player will ever be bigger than the Babe.

NUMBERS, NUMBERS

Ruth was not just a slugger, either. He had a .342 career batting average and even stole 123 bases. He led the AL in RBI five times and runs eight times. Ruth's slugging average of .690 is well ahead of Ted Williams in second place.

HANK AARON

BRAVES • BREWERS

This great slugger not only battled pitchers, but he took on a legend . . . and some nasty people. In the 1950s, Hank Aaron got his start playing baseball in the Negro Leagues. Most Major League teams did not hire African Americans, and he wanted to play! But his power soon got him a spot in the Majors with the Milwaukee Braves. He quickly became an All-Star, but his 1957 season really put him on the homer map. Aaron led the NL with 44 dingers and helped the Braves win the World Series.

That big season started a steady career of solid power. Aaron had 14 seasons with 30 or more home runs. He was a great all-around player, too. In almost every season in the 1960s, he stole 20 or more bases. His lifetime batting average is .305 and he won three Gold Gloves.

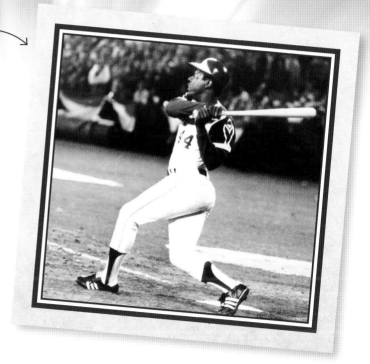

The top batting star in each league is given the Hank Aaron Award, named for this Hall of Fame home run hero.

"Hammerin' Hank" is tied with Willie Mays for the most All-Star Game appearances with 24. The Braves moved to Atlanta in 1966 and Aaron kept slugging, leading the NL that year and in 1967.

As he piled up homer after homer even into his late 30s, people began to wonder if he could catch Ruth's total of 714. By late 1973, Aaron was just a few short. Millions of fans were awaiting the start of the 1974 season to see him break the record. Sadly, some fans wrote him terrible letters. They didn't want to see a black player beat Ruth. Aaron worried for his family, but he kept playing, of course!

In the opening game of 1974, Aaron whacked homer No. 714 to tie the Babe. Then on April 8, 1974, in Atlanta, he slugged his 715th home run. Baseball had a new home run king! He went on to reach a career total of 755 before retiring in 1976.

NUMBERS, NUMBERS

Aaron is all-time leader in runs batted in. Here are the top five:

1. Hank Aaron, 2,297
2. Babe Ruth, 2,214
3. Alex Rodriguez, 2,086
4. Cap Anson, 2,075
5. Barry Bonds, 1,996

YOUR TOP TEN!

In this book, we listed our Top 10 in no particular order. We gave you some facts and information about each player. Now it's your turn to put the players in order. Find a pen and paper. Now make your own list! Who should be the No. 1 home run hitter of all time? How about your other nine choices? Would they be the same players? Would they be in the same order as they are in this book? Are any players missing from this book? Who would you include? In this case, do you just list them in order of how many homers they hit? It's your call!

Remember, there are no wrong answers. Every fan might have different choices in a different order. Every fan should be able to back up their choices, though. If you need more information, go online and learn. Or find other books about these great sluggers. Then discuss the choices with your friends!

THINK ABOUT THIS . . .

Here are some things to think about when making your ownTop 10 list:

• How did each player help his team win?

• How important were the homers the player hit?

• Did the player always play by the rules?

• What players did we leave off this list?

• When did he play? Has baseball changed over time?

SPORTS GLOSSARY

banned (BAND) stopped from taking part after breaking rules

batting average (BAT-ing AV-er-ij) a stat that measures how often a player gets a hit

binge (BINJ) a long, steady streak of doing the same thing over and over

Gold Gloves (GOLD GLUVS) awards given to the top fielder at each position in each league

lefties (LEFF-tees) a nickname for a lefthanded player, usually a pitcher

Most Valuable Player (MVP) (MOST VAL-yoo-ub-bull PLAY-er) an award given to the top player in each league or in a World Series

percentage (per-SENN-tehj) a measurement for how often something happens

Triple Crown (TRIPP-uhl KROWN) the feat of leading a league in home runs, RBI, and batting average in the same season

veteran (VETT-er-uhn) in this case, a player who has been a pro for many years

FIND OUT MORE

IN THE LIBRARY

Holub, Joan. *Who Was Babe Ruth?* New York,
NY: Grosset & Dunlap/Penguin, 2012.

Morrison, Jessica. *Hank Aaron: Home Run Hero.*
New York, NY: Crabtree Publishing, 2012.

Savage, Jeff. *Baseball Super Stats.* Minneapolis, MN: Lerner, 2017.

ON THE WEB

Visit our Web site for links about Top 10
home run hitters: **childsworld.com/links**

*Note to Parents, Teachers, and Librarians: We routinely verify our Web links to make
sure they are safe and active sites. So encourage your readers to check them out!*

INDEX

ABOUT THE AUTHOR

K. C. Kelley was an editor and writer for *Sports Illustrated* and the National Football League. He has written more than 150 books for young readers, mostly on sports. He lives in Santa Barbara, California. Hint: His pick for top home run hero was also a pitcher!